Cambridge **Discovery Education**™

▶ INTERACTIVE READERS

Series editor: Bob Hastings

WHAT ARE YOU AFRAID OF?
FEARS AND PHOBIAS

B1

Diane Naughton

CAMBRIDGE
UNIVERSITY PRESS

DISCOVERY
EDUCATION™

CAMBRIDGE
UNIVERSITY PRESS

University Printing House, Cambridge CB2 8BS, United Kingdom

One Liberty Plaza, 20th Floor, New York, NY 10006, USA

477 Williamstown Road, Port Melbourne, VIC 3207, Australia

4843/24, 2nd Floor, Ansari Road, Daryaganj, Delhi – 110002, India

79 Anson Road, #06–04/06, Singapore 079906

Cambridge University Press is part of the University of Cambridge.

It furthers the University's mission by disseminating knowledge in the pursuit of education, learning and research at the highest international levels of excellence.

www.cambridge.org
Information on this title: www.cambridge.org/9781107650510

© Cambridge University Press 2014

First published 2014
20 19 18 17 16 15 14 13 12 11

Printed in Dubai by Oriental Press

A catalogue record for this publication is available from the British Library

Library of Congress Cataloging in Publication Data

Naughton, Diane.
    What are you afraid of? fears and phobias / Diane Naughton.
        pages cm. — (Cambridge discovery interactive readers)
    ISBN 978-1-107-65051-0 (pbk. : alk. paper)
    1. Phobias—Juvenile literature. 2. English language—Textbooks for foreign speakers.
    3. Readers (Elementary) I. Title.

RC535.N386 20133
616.85'225—dc23

                    2013024756

ISBN 978-1-107-65051-0

Additional resources for this publication at www.cambridge.org

Layout services, art direction, book design, and photo research: Q2ABillSMITH GROUP
Editorial services: Hyphen S.A.
Audio production: CityVox, New York
Video production: Q2ABillSMITH GROUP

Contents

Before You Read: Get Ready!

Think about these things: long, dangerous snakes and big, black rats, high bridges and small elevators, traveling by plane in a storm, and doing important exams. How do you feel? Are you afraid?

Words to Know

Look at the pictures. Then complete the definitions below with the correct words.

spider   shark   vampire   ghost

1 _____ : a dead person in stories who bites people and drinks their blood

2 _____ : a small animal, often black or brown. It has eight legs

3 _____ : a very large fish with big teeth

4 _____ : a dead person who is in the world of the living

Words to Know

Read the paragraph. Then complete the sentences below with the correct highlighted words.

Sally has a terrible phobia of snakes. She hates seeing pictures of them, she doesn't like talking about them, and some nights she has a nightmare about them. If she sees a snake on TV, she screams loudly and immediately turns it off. She has never actually seen a snake, but just the idea makes her feel panic. Fortunately, she lives in the middle of London, so there isn't really much risk of her seeing a snake there. Living in the desert would be a nightmare, though, because there are a lot of dangerous snakes there. But her fear of snakes might also help her. In the desert, a phobia of snakes can help you survive because it makes you stay away from them!

1. When someone _____, he or she makes a high noise with their voice.

2. If you _____, you continue living after being in danger.

3. _____ is a terrible fear you feel suddenly. Often, you can't think or act clearly.

4. A _____ is a terrible fear of one thing. It's always there, and it's difficult to explain.

5. _____ is the possibility of something bad or dangerous happening to you.

6. A _____ is a frightening dream or something very bad that happens to you.

What Is Fear?

THERE IS PANIC IN THE STREETS. PEOPLE ARE SCREAMING FOR HELP AND RUNNING FROM THEIR HOMES IN FEAR. WHAT IS HAPPENING? IS THE WORLD COMING TO AN END?

On October 30, 1938, people in the United States and Canada turned on the radio and heard some terrible news.

Aliens have landed in New Jersey. The army fought bravely but lost the battle. Now, the aliens are moving across the country, destroying roads and bridges and taking control of towns and cities. There is black smoke everywhere, and in New York, people are throwing themselves into the river. Is everybody going to die?

On that night, about three million people believed that aliens were actually attacking Earth. Some people called the police for help while others ran away from the cities where they lived. But in fact, what they had heard was simply a radio play, *The War of the Worlds*, with the actor Orson Welles. There was no real danger at all. So why were people so afraid?

In 1938, the radio was quite a new invention, and many people believed everything they heard on it. At that time, stories and movies about aliens were becoming very popular, and many people thought it was really possible for aliens to come to Earth from other planets. Also, this happened not long before World War II. There was a general feeling of worry at that time because of the risk of war. When people are already nervous, panic can easily take control of them.

Orson Welles leading a radio play.

Why do we feel fear? It's a natural **emotion** that helps us and animals survive. When we think there is danger, the brain makes special hormones[1] that send messages to the rest of the body. The heart **beats** faster and blood moves around the body more quickly. We also make a kind of sugar called glucose. These changes make the body stronger and make us pay more attention to the things around us. Then we are ready to find the best way to survive: fight, hide, or run away.

[1] **hormone:** a chemical that helps the body to grow and change

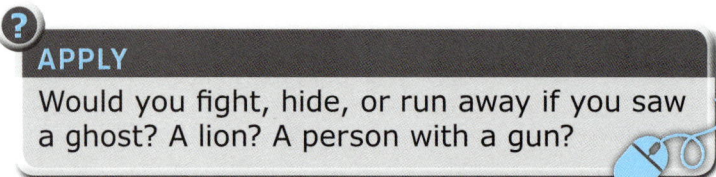

?

APPLY

Would you fight, hide, or run away if you saw a ghost? A lion? A person with a gun?

So, are we born with fear or do we learn it? In the early 20th century, the American scientist John Watson did a very famous experiment with an 11-month-old baby named Albert. A white rat was put near Albert many times and, each time, Watson made a very loud, frightening noise. This made the baby cry. Eventually, the baby learned to cry every time he saw the rat, even when there was no noise. Watson believed that Baby Albert had learned to fear rats.

Fortunately, experiments have gotten better and less cruel since then. By studying animals, scientists have shown that the fear hormone is made in a part of the brain called the amygdala.

When the danger that causes the feeling of fear disappears, the memory of that danger is kept for some time in the amygdala. So, if you are attacked and robbed in the street one night, you will probably feel nervous about walking in the street for some time after. This may be true even if you know there is no real risk. Your brain simply remembers to be afraid.

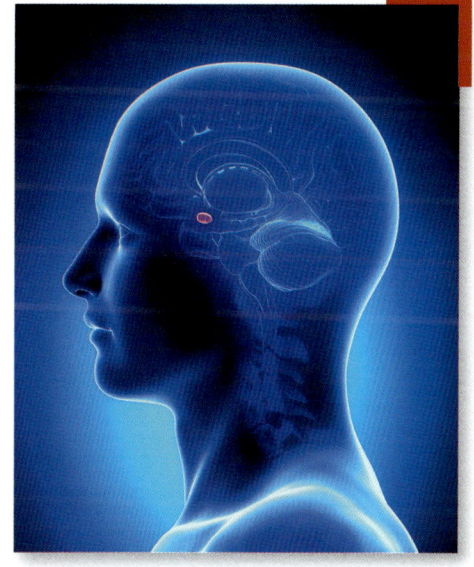

The amygdala in the brain

A tarantula

Recently, Dr. Dean Mobbs from Cambridge University has shown that the emotion of fear is experienced in two ways. Twenty people were asked to put their foot in a special box with six different parts. Then, a tarantula was put in a different part of the box from the person's foot. The people watched on video as the different parts of the box were opened, allowing the tarantula to move closer to their foot.

Mobbs found that when the spider was farther away from a person's foot, there was more activity in the part of the brain that controls emotion and worry. When the spider got nearer, the part of the brain connected with panic was more active. So, we act in different ways depending on how near danger is.

But sometimes the amygdala doesn't work in the right way. This often happens when people have had a terrible experience, for example, during a war. In this case, they think danger is always present, and they feel afraid all the time. It can cause serious health problems. Life can become a nightmare.

Fear can be a good thing. People can sometimes do amazing things when they're afraid. In 2006, for example, American Tom Boyle saw a car hit an 18-year-old boy. Tom saw that he was caught under the wheels of the car. He ran over and lifted the car up, saving the young man's life!

Fear can make people super strong.

There are also times when we feel no fear. A mother might enter a burning house to save her child, for example. Scientist Joseph Jordania calls this lack of fear *aphobia*. It can be important to help humans survive.

Parents sometimes experience aphobia when their child is in danger.

CHAPTER 2

Fear: Real or Imagined?

WHAT DIFFERENCE DOES IT MAKE IF THE THING YOU ARE AFRAID OF IS REAL OR NOT?
Toni Morrison, American author

Most people feel fear at times, but not everybody feels afraid of the same things. In 2011, scientist Daniel Treisman compared fear of crime, illnesses, and war in different European countries. He found that Spanish, Italian, and Portuguese people were more afraid in general than people from Austria or Finland. For example, 75 percent of Portuguese people said they were scared of world war, while only 28 percent of Finnish people felt the same. This fear, he says, is not connected to how likely war is but to the **culture** of the country.

In today's world, fear itself seems to be a problem. People are often afraid when there's nothing to be afraid of. Although there was 50 percent less crime in the USA in 2010 than in 1990, Americans today generally believe that crime is getting worse. People see terrible things in the news and it makes them afraid. In fact, the National Institute of Mental Health[2] says that 60 percent of our fears are connected to something that will never happen.

In the USA, 8.7 percent of people have a phobia of some kind. The most common, at 74 percent, is *glossophobia*, an extreme fear of speaking in front of an audience. Interestingly, *arachnophobia*, a fear of spiders, is a problem for 50 percent of women but only 10 percent of men. One of these men is singer Justin Timberlake.

Maybe Justin's seen a spider!

....
[2]**mental health:** the condition of the mind that shows whether someone is feeling happy, able to work, etc.

Dennis Bergkamp

But what is a phobia? It is a strong fear, even when there is no real risk. An arachnophobe (somebody with arachnophobia), for example, might not enter a room where there is a spider. Even looking at a photo of a spider can be a nightmare. And when arachnophobes actually come into contact with a spider, they feel extreme panic. They might scream or cry, and they can have problems breathing and even have heart trouble.

Ex-soccer player Dennis Bergkamp has *aerophobia*, a fear of flying. When the rest of his team flew to matches, he drove. He says, "I can't fly. I just freeze.[3] I get panicky. It starts the day before, when I can't sleep."

[3]**freeze:** suddenly stop moving, especially when you are frightened

There could be historical reasons for some phobias. *Ophidiophobia*, the fear of snakes, makes sense because snakes can be dangerous. Big animals like lions are easy to see, but snakes are often hidden.

Other people get phobias because of a personal experience. If you were bitten by a dog as a child, you might have *cynophobia* (a fear of dogs) as an adult.

In today's world, there are many new phobias like *nomophobia*, the fear of not being in contact with others by cell phone!

But if you have a phobia, remember that it is really just a story you tell yourself. Doctors say you can learn to lose this fear. If you have arachnophobia, start by looking at a photo of a spider, then look at a spider in a cage.[4] Then hold one in your hand!

[4]**cage:** a kind of box we use for keeping animals in
[5]**bacteria:** very small living things that can make people ill

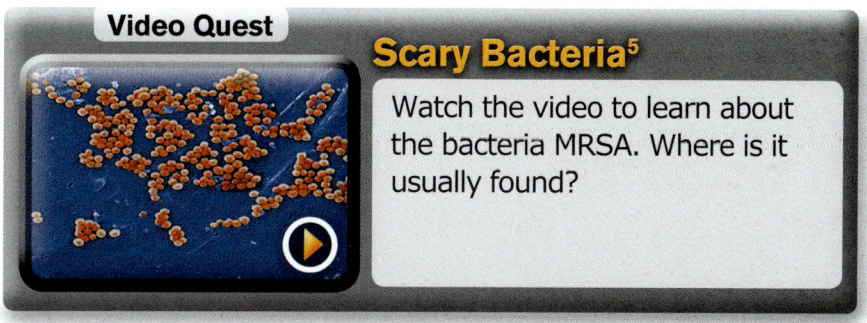

Video Quest

Scary Bacteria[5]

Watch the video to learn about the bacteria MRSA. Where is it usually found?

CHAPTER 3

The Fun of Fear

YOUR HEART IS RACING AND YOUR HANDS ARE SHAKING! IS THIS YOUR IDEA OF FUN?

Do you love walking across suspension bridges, driving your car fast, or doing extreme sports? If you like doing scary things, then you are a **thrill-seeker** – someone who looks for excitement. Some of us, it seems, are more likely to put ourselves at risk because we enjoy the strong emotions it makes us feel – the thrill of it. When we face danger, a hormone called adrenaline races around the body and gives us a feeling of great energy and excitement. We call this an **adrenaline rush**.

Long ago, life was full of dangerous moments. People lived in difficult natural environments.

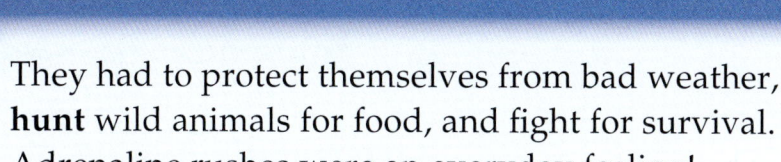

They had to protect themselves from bad weather, **hunt** wild animals for food, and fight for survival. Adrenaline rushes were an everyday feeling!

These days, many people work in offices and live in quiet neighborhoods. Life is safe. This might explain why more and more people, especially men, are doing extreme sports in their free time. They feel the need for risk. Scientist Frank Farley says, "It's the excitement. It makes things interesting, it keeps you going. When life is over, you want to look back and say, 'I lived!'"

One of these extreme sports is called free solo climbing. In this extreme sport, the climbers hold onto the rocks only with their hands and feet – they don't use **ropes**. One wrong movement and they would fall to their death.

Alain Robert, also known as the French Spiderman, is a free solo climber. Robert is famous for climbing tall buildings like the Sydney Opera House and the Eiffel Tower. But he is seeking more than thrills. He uses his spectacular climbs to bring attention to environmental problems. He is often arrested because he doesn't ask for permission to climb buildings.

In 1978, Carl Boenish started another thrill-seeking sport called BASE jumping. This is jumping from a building or high rock with a parachute. Most of the rocks or buildings are less than 600 meters high, so this means the way you jump and how quickly you open your parachute are very important. There is no time to make a mistake.

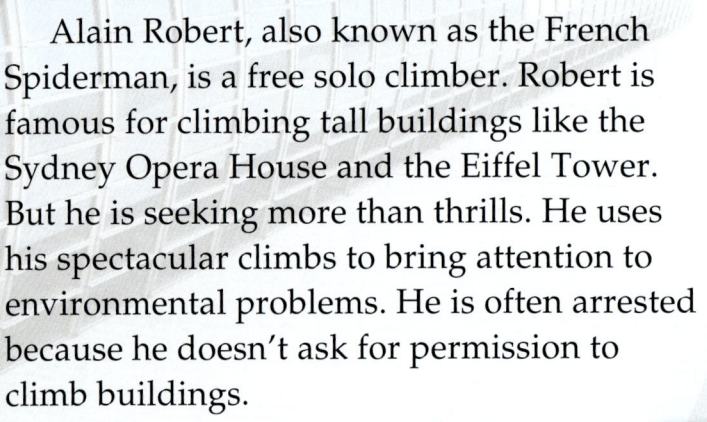

A parachute

Alain Robert climbs a building in Abu Dhabi.

18

Before 2002, about one in 60 BASE jumps ended in death. It's so risky that today it isn't allowed in most countries. Boenish himself died in 1984 while jumping off the Troll Wall in Norway.

Of course, not everybody has a safe office job. Many people take risks every day because of their work. In the USA, the most dangerous job is deep-sea fishing. For every 100,000 fishermen, about 200 of them will lose their lives at sea.

A lot of people choose to do dangerous work to help others. Many doctors and nurses risk their lives to care for people during wars or after natural disasters.[6]

[6]**disaster:** when something very bad happens that often hurts a lot of people
[7]**poison:** something that makes people ill or die if it gets into the body

BASE jumping in Rio

Video Quest

Snake Hunters

Watch this video to learn about snake hunting. What can scientists do with the poison[7]?

19

CHAPTER 4

The Business of Fear

YOU START TO PLAY THE VIDEO, AND IT'S LIKE SOMEBODY'S NIGHTMARE. THEN WHEN IT'S OVER, YOUR PHONE RINGS. SOMEONE KNOWS YOU WATCHED IT. THEY SAY, "YOU WILL DIE IN SEVEN DAYS!"

If you recognize the story above, you are probably one of the millions of people who love horror movies. These words are from the 2002 American movie *The Ring*. Becca and Katie are talking about a scary video that Katie watched a week earlier. Katie is a little afraid, but the girls manage to laugh anyway. Then strange things start happening. Will Katie really die? The audience is on the edge of their seats!

Horror movies have a history as long as cinema itself. The first one was made in 1896 by Georges Méliès. It was called *The **Haunted** Castle* and, although it was only three minutes long, it was full of typical scary things, like vampires and ghosts.

These days, horror movies are big business. Between 1995 and 2012, American horror movies made $9,093,205,812 in ticket sales alone. Traditionally, this type of movie was most popular with men, but now women choose this kind of entertainment more often than men.

BEFORE YOU DIE, YOU SEE

Another form of horror entertainment is the haunted house. There are more than 2,000 haunted house attractions in the United States. People pay as much as $60 for the fun of being scared to death!

But what happens at a haunted house? At Blackout Haunted House in New York City, visitors must go through the house alone. Inside, it's completely dark. As you walk through the rooms, scary people appear, or you feel a touch, but no one is there. Although the visitors are screaming, they know it's not real. The scary people in the house are only actors!

? EVALUATE

Why do people pay to be scared? Does it say more about our biology or modern life?

Amusement parks make money off fear as well. Roller coasters are especially good for giving people the adrenaline rush they're looking for.

Amusement parks always want to have the biggest, scariest roller coasters possible. There are thousands of roller coasters all over the world, and some of them go

On this ride, the train goes from 0 to 205 kilometers an hour in 3.5 seconds!

as fast as 240 kilometers an hour. Kingda Ka in New Jersey, USA, is the tallest. On this ride, the train goes from 0 to 205 kilometers an hour in 3.5 seconds!

Nature can be frightening, too. At Manly Sea Life Sanctuary in Sydney, Australia, people pay $200 to swim with sharks. The sharks are grey nurse sharks, which are 1–3 meters long. These sharks can only eat things that are small enough to go whole into their mouths. But it's still a thrill for people to be in the water with these dangerous animals.

Video Quest

Great Whites

Watch this video to learn about great white sharks. Why can't the shark see the box? Does it attack?

Children in Halloween costumes

The biggest scary business of all, however, is Halloween. Traditionally, this was a fun day for children to dress up in scary costumes, like a ghost, a witch, or a vampire, and go around their neighborhood collecting candy. Now, Halloween is the second biggest commercial[8] holiday of the year after Christmas. And adults love it, too!

In the past, Americans didn't spend much money between the start of school in early September and Christmas in late December. So, stores and companies started to push the idea of Halloween. It was a great success! In 2012, people spent about $8 billion on Halloween things, mostly in October.

A scary mummy costume costs about $40.

[8]**commercial:** to make money

CHAPTER 5

What Would You Do?

DO RATS MAKE YOU RUN? DO SHARKS MAKE YOU SHAKE? HOW OFTEN ARE YOU IN A PANIC?

What's Your Fear Score?

Read the questions and choose A (1 point), B (2 points), or C (3 points). Add up your points to get your score. Then read your results.

1 You're lying in bed, and you see a big spider on the ceiling. What do you do?
- Ⓐ Take a photo with your mobile phone. Cool!
- Ⓑ Calmly leave the room and get something to catch it with.
- Ⓒ Scream loudly and run out of the house in your pajamas.

2 Your friend suggests going to the mountains to try free solo climbing. What do you do?
- Ⓐ Pack your bags immediately. You can't wait to try it.
- Ⓑ Say you'll go and maybe try to climb a small mountain with ropes.
- Ⓒ Tell her she's crazy and tie yourself to a gate in case she tries to make you go.

3 You're flying, and the pilot says there's going to be a storm. What do you do?

   Ⓐ Say to yourself, "Great! This will make my trip more exciting."
   Ⓑ Feel a bit nervous, although you know it's not too dangerous.
   Ⓒ Phone a loved one in a panic. You're sure you're going to die.

4 You're watching a horror movie at home, and you suddenly hear a noise in the next room. What do you do?

   Ⓐ Continue watching TV. It can't be anything important.
   Ⓑ Feel nervous and turn off the TV so you can listen carefully.
   Ⓒ Phone the police and tell them you're being attacked by vampires.

5 You're on vacation in another country, and your cell phone doesn't work. What do you do?

   Ⓐ Think to yourself, "Great. My vacation will be more relaxing."
   Ⓑ Take your phone to a shop the next day to get it repaired.
   Ⓒ Run to the nearest shop and buy a new one.

Your Results

5–8: You're a very brave person who isn't afraid of new experiences or taking risks. In fact, you probably enjoy being afraid!

9–11: Some things scare you, but you usually manage to keep calm. Your amygdala seems to be working perfectly!

12–15: Oh, dear! Are you hiding under the bed at this moment? Remember, the world can be scary, but it's not really that bad!

?

ANALYZE

Do you think your results are correct for you? Why or why not? Think of examples to support your ideas.

After You Read

Correctly complete each sentence by choosing Ⓐ, Ⓑ, Ⓒ, or Ⓓ.

1 In 1938 in the USA, many people _____.

  Ⓐ told the police they had seen aliens

  Ⓑ thought a radio play was really true

  Ⓒ believed a world war had started

  Ⓓ said that they had been attacked

2 In an experiment at Cambridge University, some people _____.

  Ⓐ saw a big spider come nearer

  Ⓑ watched a movie about spiders

  Ⓒ touched a spider with their foot

  Ⓓ took a large spider out of a box

3 After Tim Boyle saw a car accident, he _____.

  Ⓐ called the police

  Ⓑ hit the driver

  Ⓒ drove away

  Ⓓ got stronger

4 More than half the things Americans are afraid of _____.

  Ⓐ happened in the past

  Ⓑ happened to a friend

  Ⓒ probably won't happen

  Ⓓ will probably happen

5 The phobias that people have today are sometimes connected to _____.

  Ⓐ the past

  Ⓑ the future

  Ⓒ television

  Ⓓ medicine

6 People who do solo free climbing _____ .

- Ⓐ use ropes
- Ⓑ risk their lives
- Ⓒ use parachutes
- Ⓓ only climb buildings

7 You aren't allowed to go through Blackout Haunted House _____ .

- Ⓐ carrying a bag
- Ⓑ with other people
- Ⓒ if you are an adult
- Ⓓ unless it's at night

Complete the Text

Use the words in the box to complete the text.

beating	blood	ghosts	haunted
horror	nightmare	panic	survives

Last Saturday, I went to see a **1** _____ movie. The action takes place in a **2** _____ house. A young family has just moved there, and at first they are happy. But then, the little girl starts seeing **3** _____. Some of them are covered in **4** _____, and others have no heads. She is very frightened and tells the rest of her family, but they don't believe her. Then people start dying. In the end, only the little girl **5** _____.

The next night, I had a terrible **6** _____. I woke up, and my heart was **7** _____ so fast that I jumped out of bed in a **8** _____. I think I'll see a romantic movie next week!

How About You?

Which of the scary activities from the book would you like to do? Which would you NOT like to do? Why?

Answer Key

Words to Know, page 4
1 vampire **2** spider **3** shark **4** ghost

Words to Know, page 5
1 screams **2** survive **3** Panic **4** phobia **5** Risk
6 nightmare

Apply, page 8
Answers will vary.

Video Quest, page 15
MRSA is usually found in hospitals.

Video Quest, page 19
If a tiger snake bites you, you have breathing problems, and you can't move your body. You may die. Scientists make important medicine from the poison.

Evaluate, page 21
Answers will vary.

Video Quest, page 22
The shark can't see the box because it isn't colored. It doesn't attack.

Analyze, page 25
Answers will vary.

Choose the Correct Answers, page 26
1 B **2** A **3** D **4** C **5** A **6** B **7** B

Complete the Text, page 27
1 horror **2** haunted **3** ghosts **4** blood **5** survives
6 nightmare **7** beating **8** panic

How About You?, page 27
Answers will vary.